AUNT TAM'S
FAMILY RECIPES
AND STORIES WORTH TELLING

Tammy Buzzetti

Published 2020
Printed in the United States of America

978-1734867206 (p)
978-1734867220 (h)
978-1734867213 (e)

Canoe Tree Press
4697 Main Street
Manchester, VT 05255

www.CanoeTreePress.com

To my children Anthony,
Hunter and Ruby
Thank you for always eating
everything I put in front of you.
This book is for you.
Love, Mom

Don't worry about bite'n off
more'n you can chew.
Your mouth is probably a whole
lot bigger'n you think!

TABLE OF CONTENTS

INTRODUCTION

I am a crazy busy business owner, wife, mother of three amazing children, and an over the top volunteer who LOVES TO COOK. My cooking is for the people I love and every recipe has a story, family member, or tradition behind it. I hope you all love them as much as my family and I do.

I am blessed to live in a beautiful ranching community at the base of the majestic Ruby Mountains, but it's a 10-mile drive to the nearest grocery store and that can be a real pain. I have learned to improvise a lot in recipes, and my sister says I can make an amazing meal out of nothing. I was motivated to write this cookbook when members of my family and friends were always asking me over and over for my recipes. But to put them down on paper with exact amounts of ingredients proved to be challenging. Yep, I am one of those cooks that puts some of this, a little bit of that and voilà! Dinner! So I did a test run on all these recipes and wrote down the amounts, but feel free to add your personal touch, a little of this or some of that, as you please.

With our busy lives we need flexible recipes, or make it exactly how its written either way, I know it will turn out amazing and before you know it your family will be asking you for the recipes. I love preparing these recipes for and with my family and friends. I hope you love doing the same.

—Tammy

CHAPTER 1: COCKTAILS

I love a good cocktail!!!

My family and friends get together to celebrate birthdays, holidays or any reason we can find to celebrate. I hope you enjoy these recipes as much as we do. We live at 5,500-feet elevation in what is considered the high desert, so we get extreme cold, snow, and winter big time. But in the summer, it can be 100 degrees and dry. Therefore theses recipes are from hot toddies to ice cold refreshing beverages. Drinks for all seasons!

Russian Tea

1 cup white sugar
2 cups Tang powder drink mix
1 cup instant tea mix with lemon
2 tsp cinnamon
1 tsp ground cloves
1/2 tsp nutmeg
1 jigger (shot) whiskey, brandy, or vodka

MIXOLOGY

Mix all ingredients together in a mixing bowl with a whisk. Using a funnel pour mixture in an airtight container. I use a large Mason jar. Then in 8 ounces of hot or cold water add 2 heaping tablespoons of dry mixture, add more if you like. I make juice by the glass over ice in the summer with this mix and you can dress it up with a slice of an orange for company. In the winter I love drinking it hot. It's warm delicious goodness hits the spot and with a full day supply of vitamin C it can help keep the crud away. For medicinal purposes of course (wink wink) you can add a jigger (shot) of vodka in the summer and brandy or whiskey in the winter, and throw a cinnamon stick in for good measure.

ENJOY

Apricot Margarita

6 ounces or 3/4 cup tequila
1 6-oz can frozen limeade
2 ounces or 1/4 cup apricot brandy
3 large apricots, ripe or canned
Ice

MIXOLOGY

In a large blender add the 4 ingredients and then fill the blender to the top with ice. If you would like, you can dampen the edge of your favorite glass with a lime wedge and dip into a bowl of sugar or salt depending on your mood to coat the rim. Fill glass to the top and garnish with a lime wedge, or drink straight from the blender pitcher, depending on what kind of day you are having. HAHAHA

These are so crazy delicious and are a huge crowd pleaser, so you must be able to drink them year round. So use canned apricots if you don't have fresh ones. You can use any apricot liqueur if you don't like or have apricot brandy. I just like the warm, fuzzy feeling brandy gives me deep inside. It's like a big old hug. If you want to make fizzy margaritas, just add a splash of apricot or lime flavored sparkling water.

I do suggest using high quality tequila, my personal favorite is Patron Silver. It can mean the difference between having a hangover and NOT having a hangover. I have found I enjoy this drink most when surrounded by my closest female friends and family.

Tom & Jerry

6 egg whites
1/2 tsp cream of tarter
2 cups powdered sugar
6 egg yolks
2 cups powdered sugar
1/2 tsp cinnamon
1/2 tsp allspice
1/2 tsp nutmeg
1/4 tsp cloves
1 can sweetened condensed milk
2 tsp vanilla
1 jigger (shot) rum
1 jigger (shot) brandy

MIXOLOGY

Whip first 2 ingredients with an electric mixer on high until stiff peaks form. I use my stand mixer just because its easier but any mixer will do. In a second bowl mix the next 8 ingredients. Then fold the fluffy egg whites into other ingredients. Store this batter in your refrigerator for 7-10 days in an airtight container. It may separate slightly but just mix it up before using and it will be fine.

To make: put 2 heaping tablespoons of this gooey goodness into 6 ounces of hot water or milk. I do half water, half milk, add jiggers of rum and brandy, and stir well with a spoon until all batter is dissolved. It will be all deliciously foamy. Then sprinkle with nutmeg and share with any surprise company that might stop by on a chilly night.

Hot Buttered Rum

1 pound butter (4 sticks)
1 qt vanilla bean ice cream
1 pound brown sugar
1 pound powdered sugar
1 tbsp cinnamon
1 tsp ground cloves
1 tsp nutmeg
Spiced rum

MIXOLOGY

Soften butter and ice cream. I leave them out on the counter for an hour or so, or I zap them in the microwave for 30 to 60 seconds. Then add them to the mixer and mix on low speed until combined. I use a stand mixer because its easier but you can use a whisk and a bowl for this recipe. Add all other ingredients except rum. Transfer mixture to a freezer safe container with a lid. Store in the freezer until ready to make cocktail. The mixture stays soft even in the freezer.

To make: add 1 or 2 heaping tablespoon of mixture (depending on how sweet you like it; I like 2) to 6 ounces of boiling water. Stir until mix is dissolved, then add 1 jigger or more (wink wink) of spiced rum. You can garnish with a sprinkle of nutmeg and a cinnamon stick if you like.

We drink this a lot in the winter when we get home from a snowmobile ride. It's the perfect way to warm up. The kids like it too, just make it for them minus the rum, or try it as a nightcap and sleep like a baby. I have made this with different combos of sugars—brown, white and powdered, when I didn't have enough of one or the other and I wasn't driving all the way to the store to get it. It always is still amazing and trust me any rum will do, too.

Warning: if you serve these to your friends and family, they keep coming back for more. HAHAHA!

Jingle Jangle Juice

2 quarts orange juice
2 quarts cranberry juice
1 quart pineapple juice
1 cup powdered fruit punch mix
1 liter ginger ale
2 cups spiced rum
2 cups cranberry vodka
1 cup fresh cranberries
2 oranges sliced
4 cinnamon sticks
Ice

MIXOLOGY

This recipe is for a party with a large crowd. I make this every year for the annual Buzzetti Bash Christmas Party. Start with a large punch container that holds at least 2 gallons of liquid. Pour all the ingredients in and mix with a large spoon. Then add the orange slices, (word to the wise, make sure you removed all the seeds from the oranges they plug up the spouts on the beverage containers and yes I learned this the hard way) cranberries, and cinnamon sticks. Give it another stir, then add ice to the top of the container. You can really use any fruit juices with this recipe and any Vodka or Rum. You can also use lemon lime soda instead of ginger ale. You can serve this punch over ice or in a champagne flute it is delicious either way, but it does pack a punch! HaHaHa couldn't resist.

Sangria

1 bottle wine (any)
1 cup fruit juice (orange, apple,
cranberry, pineapple etc.)
1/2 cup alcohol (brandy, whiskey, vodka etc.)
1/3 cup sugar
1 cup fruit (any fruit fresh or frozen)

MIXOLOGY

Just remember 5 ingredients is all you need to make an amazing
Sangria! Wine, juice, alcohol, sugar, fruit. In a large glass pitcher pour
in sugar, juice, alcohol and stir well. Then add bottle of wine and fruit.
Stir and refrigerate for a minimum of 1 hour but 6-8 hours is best.
To serve remove from from refrigerator and stir well. Pour over
ice, if you like some fizz top with club soda its delicious.

Irish Mule

Ice
Ginger beer
Limes
Irish whiskey

MIXOLOGY

Fill a beautiful copper mug full of ice. Add 1 jigger (shot) of Irish Whiskey
and squeeze the juice of 1/2 of a lime cut in 2 wedges in the mug then
drop the lime wedges in. Fill to the top with ginger beer mix well.
This drink is delicious and refreshing and according to our friend Roger, if you
drink a couple three of these with friends before church on Christmas Eve
you might sing louder than normal and take a nap in church. HAHAHA

ENJOY

Bloody Caesar

1 cup Clamato
1 jigger(shot) vodka
4 dashes Worcestershire sauce
2 dashes Tabasco sauce
1/2 teaspoon celery salt
1/4 teaspoon horseradish
3 green olives
1 celery stick
1 lime wedge

MIXOLOGY

I love this spicy version of a Bloody Mary. Fill a tall glass with ice, add Clamato, vodka, Worcestershire, Tabasco, celery salt, horseradish stir until thoroughly mixed. Then add olives, a lime wedge, and a celery stick. Give it another quick stir with the celery stick. This is a delicious drink and a snack all in one. I started making these at Thanksgiving 11 years ago, and they are still a family favorite.

CHAPTER 2: APPETIZERS
Did someone say football?

We host a Super Bowl party every year, and I make a ton of appetizers for it. I like having the supplies on hand for appetizers so if someone stops by I can throw something together really quick. I have learned that people will always eat if you put food in front of them, even when they say they are not hungry. HAHAHA

Deviled Eggs

1 dozen hard boiled eggs
1/2 tsp onion powder
1/2 tsp garlic powder
1/2 tsp salt
1/2 tsp pepper
1/2 tsp paprika
3 dashes hot sauce
3 dashes Worcestershire sauce
1/2 cup mayonnaise
1/3 cup sour cream
1 tsp mustard

Peel hard boiled eggs and cut them in half. Place egg whites on a platter and egg yokes in a bowl. Mash egg yokes with a fork, and add all remaining ingredients. I whip mine with an emulsion blender but you can use a whisk and elbow grease also. I put the yummy fluffy yellow goodness into a piping bag and fill the whites very full and then sprinkle with more paprika to make them pretty.

My family eats these almost faster than I can make them. They are absolutely delicious. You can make these ahead of time and refrigerate in an airtight container that won't squish them or make your refrigerator smell like eggs.

ENJOY

Cowboy Caviar

1 15-oz can pinto beans
1 15-oz can black beans
1 cup canned corn
1 cup chopped tomatoes
1 cup chopped avocado
1 cup of diced green, orange, or yellow peppers
2 tsp minced garlic
2/3 cup chopped cilantro
1 jalapeño seeded and diced
1/4 cup diced red onion
2 tsp chili powder
1 tsp cumin
1 tsp salt
1/2 tsp black pepper
4 tbsp olive oil
Juice 1 lime

This dip is a crowd pleaser. I just mix all the ingredients together and serve with tortilla chips. It is a healthy dip full of veggies and goodness.

ENJOY

Cabbage Dip

1 head of cabbage shredded
1 large bunch of cilantro
2 large tomatoes chopped
1 avocado chopped
1/4 red onion diced
1/2 diced jalapeño seeded
1 diced clove garlic
1 tsp salt
1 tsp sugar
Juice of 2 limes

Mix all ingredients well in a large bowl. Serve with corn chips.
I have had many people ask me for this recipe it is super good!

Table Guacamole

4 ripe avocados
1/4 cup finely chopped red onion
1 large Roma tomato
2 tbsp finely chopped cilantro
1/2- jalapeno minced
1 clove minced garlic
Juice of 1 lime
1 tsp salt

Smash the avocados in a bowl, add remaining ingredients
and mix well. This is best eaten when first made.

Clam Dip

1 can minced clams drained
2 cups sour cream
2 tsp Worcestershire sauce
1 tsp minced garlic
1 tsp salt
4 dashes hot sauce
1/2 tsp lemon juice

In medium mixing bowl stir clams and sour cream together. Add remaining ingredients stir well. I love this with Lays classic potato chips.

My dad loves clam dip. He brings it to most family get togethers. It's his favorite.

Carmel Corn

1/2 cup butter
2 cups brown sugar
1 cup light corn syrup
1 15-oz can sweetened condensed milk
1 tsp vanilla
1 extra large bowl of air popped popcorn (approximately 10 quarts)

In a saucepan over medium heat melt butter, then add brown sugar, corn syrup, and condensed milk. Stirring constantly until combined. When it starts to bubble around the edges remove from heat add vanilla mix well and pour over popcorn.

My family loves this delicious treat. It is a great caramel because it stays soft and chewy. It also isn't overly sweet so its easy to eat the whole bowl before you know it. I am speaking from experience. HAHAHA

ENJOY

Sweet & Spicy Nuts

1/4 cup butter
1 tbsp cinnamon
1/4 tsp nutmeg
1/4 tsp cloves
1/4 tsp allspice
2 tsp chili powder
2 tsp salt
1 tbsp brown sugar
3 cups your favorite nuts
Preheat oven to 350 degrees.

Line baking sheet with aluminum foil. In a large cast iron pan over medium heat combine butter, spices, sugar and nuts. Mix until all butter is melted and spice mixture has coated all the nuts evenly. Spread the nuts evenly on baking sheet and bake for 15 minutes. Remove from oven and let cool. These are totally delicious warm but even when cold I still eat them by the hand full. They are a great treat to give to neighbors at the holidays. I have used mixed nuts, almonds or pecans. They are all delicious. If you want to heat up the spice you can use cayenne in place of chili powder.

I buy roasted nuts every time I am in a store where they have them they are a real treat. I decided to come up with my own recipe a few years ago and make them for the holidays. They were a huge hit and I make them often now.

8 cups air popped popcorn
1/2 tsp rosemary
1/2 tsp Italian seasoning
1 tsp garlic salt
1/2 tsp black pepper
1 tsp salt
2 tbsp olive oil
2 tbsp butter
1/4 parmesan cheese

Savory Popcorn

Pop the popcorn into a large bowl and set aside. In a small saucepan melt butter over medium heat. Add olive oil, rosemary, pepper and garlic salt stir well. Remove from heat and pour over popcorn. Toss popcorn until evenly coated, then add cheese and toss again.

I had popcorn like this the first time from a food truck. I came home on a mission to remake it. This is the version I came up with and we all love it.

ENJOY

Jalapeño Poppers

12 jalapeño peppers
1 8-oz block cream cheese
1 cup cheddar cheese
1 tsp onion powder
1 tsp minced garlic
1/2 tsp salt
1/2 tsp pepper
6 slices of bacon

Preheat oven to 400 degrees.

Line a baking sheet with aluminum foil and coat with nonstick spray. Cut the peppers in half and clean out seeds and ribs. Place halved peppers on baking sheet. In a medium bowl mix cream cheese, onion powder, minced garlic, cheddar cheese, salt and pepper. Fill pepper halves full of mixture. Cut bacon slices the same length as the pepper halves long ways. Place bacon on top of peppers and bake for 25 minutes or until bacon is crisp.

My son Hunter loves these poppers. He makes them and eats most of them we are lucky if we get one. HAHAHA

ENJOY

CHAPTER 3:
SOUPS & SUCH
Comfort Food Coming Up!!!

Yummy in my tummy. Let's face it I find ALL food comforting, true fact. But there is something about a hot bowl full of goodness especially on a cold day that just soothes the soul and warms the heart. Make these recipes for the ones you love and soon you will be the one they come to for comfort. That expression "the way to the heart is through the stomach" is absolutely 100% true.

Ham & Beans

1 1/2 cups ham
4 cups lima beans
1 small yellow onion
4 cups chicken broth
1 tsp cumin
1 tbsp minced garlic
1 tsp black pepper
4 tbsp butter
1 tbsp bacon grease (optional)

OK disclaimer! I usually make this when I have left over ham from a holiday, but you can make it any time. I take the left over ham and cut what I can up in small pieces. Add the ham bone and pieces to the crockpot if I am making it in the morning for dinner but if I have an hour I put in in a pot on the stove. Then I add the beans. You can use dried lima beans and pre-soak them or you can use canned Lima beans and rinse and drain them. Then add remaining ingredients. If I know I am going to put this in the crockpot in the morning for dinner I make bacon for breakfast and add the grease to the crockpot also just for some extra goodness, but its not necessary. Cook in crockpot for 6-8 hours or if in a pot on the stove bring it to a boil then turn it down to medium put a lid on it and let it simmer for 45 minutes and then stir it up and dish it up in a large bowl.

Beef Stew

2 pounds of beef stew meat
4 tbsp butter
2 cups yellow onion chopped in big chunks
2 cups coarsely chopped carrots
2 cups coarsely chopped celery
4 medium sized quartered potatoes
1 tbsp minced garlic
2 packages stew seasoning mix
2 tsp salt
2 tsp coarse pepper
4 cups of water

Most of the time when I make this I put it all in the crockpot in the morning and cook it all day on low for dinner. But if I only have an hour I put it on the stove top in my dutch oven. I brown the meat on hi heat, add the onion, garlic, seasonings, vegetables. Then add water bring it to a boil. Reduce heat to medium put the lid on and cook for 45 minutes stirring every 15 minutes. This is easy hearty delicious stew that my family gobbles up and I'm positive your family will too.

ENJOY

Tuscan Soup

1 medium yellow onion
1 tbsp minced garlic
29-oz can of pumpkin puree
15-oz can of tomato sauce
2 tsp honey
2 cups chicken stock
1/4 tsp cinnamon
2 tsp salt
1/2 cup full fat coconut milk from can
1 tsp rosemary
1/2 tsp sage
1 tsp pepper

Add all ingredients to a slow cooker except coconut milk stir together
and cook on high for 4 hours or low for 8 hours. Before serving add
coconut milk and use an emulsion blender and blend in slow cooker until
very smooth. Ladle into bowl and sprinkle with parmesan cheese.

I discovered a similar recipe when I was on the whole 30 diet once. This recipe is
super easy to modify also. I have used a bunch of tomatoes I had that were going
to go bad in place of the canned tomatoes sauce. I have used regular milk in place
of coconut milk also. It is always delicious no mater what. My family loves it.

Chicken Noodle Soup

NOODLES

1 egg per person
1 cup of flour per egg
1/4 tsp salt per egg
1 tbsp milk per egg
1 tbsp melted butter per egg

In a large bowl stir salt and flour together. In a medium bowl whisk eggs. Add eggs, milk, and butter to flour. Mix with a fork at first and then change to your hands. Knead dough on a floured surface until smooth. Roll out into a rectangle until the dough is 1/4 inch thick. Cut into 1/4 to 1/2 inch strips with pizza cutter. Leave on counter to dry.

SOUP

2 large chicken breasts or 2 1/2 cups shredded chicken
1 cup yellow onion diced
1 cup diced celery
1 cup diced carrots
2 tbsp butter
1 tsp salt
1 tsp pepper
1 tsp thyme
4 dashes hot sauce
8 cups chicken broth

In a large dutch oven or stock pot over medium heat on top of the stove melt butter and add chicken breasts. Cover with lid and cook on each side for 10 minutes. Remove chicken breasts onto a cutting board and let cool. Add onion, celery, carrots to the pot and continue to cook over medium heat until onions are soft. Add salt, pepper, thyme, broth, and hot sauce. Turn up to medium-high heat and cover with lid. While waiting for that to boil shred chicken with 2 forks and add chicken back to the pot. Once the soup has come to a rolling boil slowly add egg noodles and cook for 10 minutes stirring every few minutes to keep egg noodles from sticking together. Remove from heat and ladle into soup bowls.

This soup is always requested when anyone in the family is feeling under the weather. It always makes everyone feel better. It is a true comfort food.

Mac & Cheese

2 1/2 cups pasta (large shells, macaroni, bowtie)
1 cup chicken broth
2 cups water
1 tsp salt
1 tsp pepper
1 tsp garlic powder
4 tbsp butter
1 cup grated sharp cheddar cheese
1 1/2 cups Velveeta cheese in cubes
2/3 cups milk

This is a recipe intended for the insta-pot but I will tell
you how to cook it on the stove top also.

Insta-pot recipe: add macaroni, broth, water, salt, pepper, garlic
powder, and butter to insta-pot and cook for 6 to 8 minutes. Then
release steam and stir pasta, put insta-pot on warm and add in cheeses
and milk continue to stir until cheese is completely melted.

Stove top recipe: cook pasta according to package directions. In dutch oven or large
pot on stove top on medium heat add broth, salt, pepper, garlic powder, butter, milk.
Bring to a boil and add cheeses stirring constantly until completely melted. Remove
from heat and stir in pasta until all pasta is completely coated in cheesy goodness.

I have made this for many parties and family gatherings where I double
the recipe and I have had many guests try to leave with my insta-pot or
dutch oven only to realize there is never any left over. HAHAHA

Cheesy Potatoes

1 32-oz bag frozen shredded potatoes
1 tbsp dried chives
2 cups sour cream
1 tsp garlic powder
4 tbsp melted butter
2 1/2 cups shredded cheddar cheese
1 cup milk
1 tsp salt & pepper

Preheat oven to 350 degrees.

Mix all ingredients in large bowl. Spread evenly in a 9x13
baking dish. Bake for 35-40 minutes until all bubbly.

These potatoes are my sister-in-law Adrienne's favorite. They are deliciously cheesy.

Scalloped Potatoes

8 cups peeled and thinly sliced potatoes
1 can cream of mushroom soup
1 can cheese soup
2 cans of milk
1/2 cup finely chopped onion
1 tsp salt & pepper

Preheat oven to 350 degrees.

Mix all ingredients together in large bowl. Spread evenly in 9x13 baking dish. Bake for the first 30 minutes covered with foil, then remove foil and bake another 30 minutes. Until all bubbly and top is golden brown.

This was my mom's recipe, we had it at Christmas and Easter a lot growing up. It is very creamy and cheesy and it pairs well with ham or beef.

Yummy Yams

2 apples cored, peeled, and sliced
1/3 chopped pecans
1/2 brown sugar
1 tsp cinnamon
2 17-oz cans yams, drained
1/2 cup butter
3 cups miniature marshmallows

Toss apples, nuts, brown sugar, cinnamon, and yams in a large bowl. Spread into 9x11 baking dish and dot top with butter cover with foil and bake for 35-40 minutes in 350 degree oven. Remove foil and spread marshmallows all over the top. Return to oven for 5 minutes or until marshmallows are all puffed up.

I love this casserole! I seem to only make it on holidays but it is a delicious treat and I should make it more. My great nephew Ryle who is 2 loves it too, he calls it cake. HAHAHA

CHAPTER 4: BREADS & BISCUITS

Anything Bread Related

I love everything bread! There is nothing better than eating a warm roll right out of the oven dripping with butter, or a biscuits slathered in apple butter or raspberry preserves. All my bread recipes are easy, and delicious.

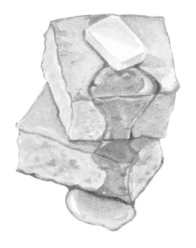

Cornbread

2 cups biscuit mix
1 cup butter
1 cup milk
1 cup yellow corn meal
1 tsp salt
1/2 tsp baking soda
2/3 cup sugar
2 eggs

Preheat oven to 350 degrees.

In a large mixing bowl mix all dry ingredients. I use my stand mixer. Then add milk, melted butter, and eggs. Pour into a greased 13 x 9 baking pan. Bake at 350 degrees for 30 minutes. Serves 12. This cornbread is moist, soft and absolutely delicious. Serve it with your favorite soup, chili, or make it for breakfast and serve with maple syrup, butter, and sausage.

My good friend Dawn shared this recipe with me, God love her! It is hands down the best cornbread ever! Now I am sharing it with you.

ENJOY

Banana Nut Bread

1 yellow cake mix
1 small box instant banana pudding
1/2 cup water
1/2 cup vegetable oil
3 ripe bananas mashed
4 eggs
3/4 cup chopped walnuts

Preheat oven to 350 degrees.

In mixing bowl mash bananas. I use my stand mixer to make it easier but you don't have to you can use a large bowl and a whisk. After bananas are well mashed, add remaining ingredients and mix well. Divide batter between 2 loaf pans. Grease and flour pans or line with foil or parchment paper for easy removal of loaf from pan. Bake at 350 degrees in oven for 40 minutes. This recipe is great to make ahead, you can freeze and then thaw the loaves, they stay moist and delicious.

My daughter Ruby loves "nana" bread. Every time you have some bananas getting brown and you don't have time to make them into bread right then. Peel them and put them in a zip lock bag in the freezer. You can thaw them out for bread when you have time or you can easily use them in smoothies also.

Mom's Butterhorn Rolls

2 packages yeast
1/2 cup water
1 cup milk
1/4 sugar
1 tsp salt
1/4 butter (plus more for brushing)
3 eggs
4 cups flour

Dissolve yeast in lukewarm water and set aside in small bowl. In 4 quart dutch oven on stove top over medium heat scald milk. Then remove from heat add butter, stir until melted. Add sugar and salt, stir until sugar is dissolved. If this mixture is warm but not hot you can continue with the following steps, but if it is still hot continue to stir until it is just warm. Pour into stand mixer with dough hook. Turn mixer to low, add yeast mixture, 1 cups of flour, and eggs one at a time mix well. Add remaining 3 cups of flour, mix until soft dough forms. Place dough in large greased bowl cover with plastic wrap and put in warm place. Let dough raise until doubled usually about 45 to 60 minutes. Then remove plastic wrap and punch down dough. This is a great way to relieve stress at the holidays hahaha. Divide dough in half and one half at a time roll dough out into a 12" circle on lightly floured surface. Brush surface of dough circle with melted butter. Using a pizza cutter, cut dough circle like a pizza into 8 equal slices or triangles. Roll up each triangle starting at the outside edge. Place rolls in a buttered 13 x 9 pan. Repeat with other half of dough. You should have 4 rows of 4 rolls so a total of 16 rolls. Brush tops of rolls with melted butter. Cover loosely with dish towel and place in warm place until rolls almost double in size which is usually 30 minutes.

Preheat oven to 375 degrees. When rolls are raised, bake for 15-20 minutes or until golden brown. Remove rolls from oven, and guess what? Yep, one more time brush with melted butter.

These are best served right out of the oven or there wont be any left by the time you serve dinner they have a way of disappearing quickly. I double this recipe when I make it for my large family get togethers at the holidays and it still comes out beautifully every time. This is my mom's recipe. I made these rolls for every holiday meal with her growing up and I cherish those memories. I have continued that tradition of making these rolls with my family. These rolls are a heavenly treat from our angel.

Zucchini Bread

3 eggs
2 cups sugar
1 tbsp vanilla
1 cup vegetable oil
2 cups shredded zucchini
2 cups flour
1 tsp baking powder
1 tsp salt
1 tbsp cinnamon
1 cup chopped walnuts

Mix eggs, sugar, vanilla, and oil. I use my stand mixer, but you can use a large bowl and a whisk. Add flour, baking powder, salt, and cinnamon mix well and then add nuts and mix until combined. Grease and flour pans. Divide between 2 regular size loaf pans or one bunt pan. Bake at 350 degrees for 50-60 minutes.

This is one of my favorite breads. It's a real treat, you can add chocolate chips to it if you want or replace the vegetable oil with apple sauce for a healthier version.

Soft Gingerbread

2/3 cup sugar
1/2 cup butter
2 eggs
3/4 cup molasses
3/4 cup milk
2 cups flour
2 tbsp baking powder
1 tsp baking soda
1 tsp salt
1 tsp ginger
1 tsp cloves
1 tsp allspice
2 tsp cinnamon

This moist delicious cake is just amazing. I was obsessed with this recipe when I first started making it. I made it for friends and family every time we had a get together because it was always such a big hit. With an electric mixer mix sugar, softened butter, eggs, molasses, and milk until well combined. Then add flour, baking powder, baking soda, salt, and spices and mix until well combined. Pour into 9x9 greased baking pan. Bake at 350 degrees for 35-40 minutes. Top with heavy whipped cream.

I love taking this to a friend or family member who is experiencing a bump in the road of life. There is something about gingerbread that just makes you heart lighter. It always puts smiles on faces. Try it, you will see.

ENJOY

Buttermilk Biscuits

2 1/4 cups flour
1 tbsp baking powder
1 tsp salt
1 tbsp sugar
1/3 cup butter or shortening
1 cup buttermilk or milk

Preheat oven to 425 degrees.

Stir dry ingredients together in a bowl. Then with a knife cut the cubed cold butter into thin slices. Add them to dry mixture and with a fork or pasty cutter combine until the mixture looks like white peas. Then add buttermilk, but I make buttermilk substitute all the time which is 1 tbsp vinegar added to the 1 cup of milk. Mix it up and let it sit for about 5 minutes. Mix and turn out on floured surface. Dust with flour and knead until easy to handle. Pat out in a 1 inch thick circle, then use a biscuit cutter to cut biscuits. I put the biscuits onto a baking sheet with a baking mat on it. Brush the tops with melted butter and bake for 13-15 minutes.

These biscuits are easy, delicious and come out perfect every time.

ENJOY

Sour Cream Biscuits

2 1/2 cups Biscuit mix (Bisquick)
1/2 cup sour cream
1/2 cup club soda
1/4 cup melted butter

Preheat oven to 450 degrees.

Mix all ingredients together and turn out onto flour surface. Dust with flour and knead until easy to handle. Pat into circle 1 inch thick. Melt butter in microwave and pour into 9x9 baking dish. Cut biscuits with biscuit cutter and place in baking dish coating both sides with butter. Bake for 10-13 minutes.

These biscuits are soft, fluffy, delicate, and oh so delightful.

Sausage Gravy

1 pound pork breakfast sausage
3 tbsp butter
1/4 cup flour
3 cups milk
2 tsp salt
1 tsp black pepper
1/4 tsp ground sage

You can't have biscuits without gravy!!!! In a saucepan brown sausage over medium heat until crumbly. Add the butter to sausage, then add the flour. Mix well, then add milk, salt, pepper and sage. Cook over medium heat until thickened, stirring often. Pour over biscuits.

Easy Cake Doughnuts

2 cups biscuit mix
2 tbsp sugar
1 tsp vanilla
1 egg
1/4 cup milk
1/4 tsp cinnamon
1/4 tsp nutmeg

Heat oil in pan or fryer to 375 degrees.

Mix all ingredients together until smooth. Turn dough out onto floured surface dust with flour and knead until dough is easy to handle. then roll out until 1/2 inch thick and cut out doughnuts with a doughnut cutter. Carefully drop doughnuts into hot oil. Cook doughnut for 1 minute on each side or until golden brown. Remove from oil and place on paper towels to drain. Or bake them at at 375 degree oven for 10-13 minutes. Mix up easy chocolate icing because everything is better with chocolate. Melt 1/4 cup semisweet chocolate chips in microwave with 3 tbsp butter for 30 seconds and stir well when smooth stir is 1 cup powdered sugar and 1 tsp vanilla. When cool enough to handle dip doughnuts in glaze.

These are so easy and so scrumptious.

Easy Yeast Doughnuts

2 cans Grand-sized biscuits
This is a total cheater recipe that I love! Roll the biscuits out in the shape
of a large maple bar. You can bake these according to the can or you can
fry them (my preference) in hot oil. Either way, they are delicious.
Once cooked put this maple icing on them:
1/4 cup butter
1/4 cup brown sugar
Melt together in saucepan on stove top on low heat. Remove from heat and add:
3 tbsp milk
1 tbsp corn syrup
2 tsp maple extract
2 cups powdered sugar

Mix well. Coat top of doughnuts with glaze.

Cinnamon Rolls

DOUGH

2 cups whole milk
1/2 cup butter
1/2 cup white sugar
1 package quick rise yeast
4 1/2 cups flour
1 tsp baking soda
1 tsp baking powder
1 tsp salt

FILLING

1/2 cups melted butter
1/2 cup sugar
1 tbsp cinnamon

FROSTING

1/2 cup softened butter
2 tsp vanilla
4 ounces softened cream cheese
4 cups powdered sugar

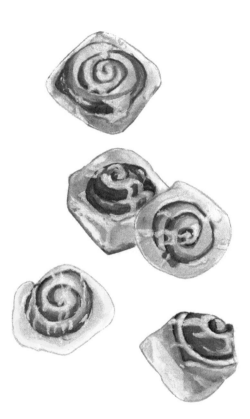

To make the dough, put milk in large dutch oven on stove top over medium heat. Dissolve sugar in milk. When milk starts to boil remove from heat and add cold cubed butter to milk stirring constantly until completely melted. At this point the milk should just be lukewarm. Sprinkle the yeast over the milk mixture and let sit for 5 minutes.

Add 4 cups of flour to milk mixture and stir with a wooden spoon until combined. Cover with lid and let rise for 30 minutes. When you remove lid mixture should be bubbly and puffed. Add the remaining 1/2 cup flour, soda, salt and baking powder to mixture. Mix well with wooden spoon.

Butter baking dish heavily. Flour surface of a large workspace. Lightly punch down dough with floured hands. Pour out onto the floured surface and dust top of dough with flour. Using floured hands and a floured rolling pin press and roll the dough into a rectangle about 30" by 18 inches. The dough will be very thin. Brush melted butter on surface of dough, then sprinkle with sugar and cinnamon.

Start rolling up dough on the 30 inch side closest to you. Gently pull the dough towards you as you roll it up into a log. Pinch the seams closed to seal. You can cut rolls into 1 inch slices with a sharp knife or use a piece of dental floss.

Preheat oven to 375. Place rolls in pan and let rise for 20 minutes. Place rolls in oven and bake for 15-20 minutes or until light golden brown. Remove from oven and place on cooling rack.

To make frosting, use an electric mixer. Cream together butter, and cream cheese. When light and fluffy add powdered sugar and vanilla.

Orange Rolls

Use the same dough recipe as the cinnamon rolls, just use the filling recipe below and pour the glaze on them right when they come out of the oven. Delicious!!!

FILLING

8 tbsp orange marmalade
1/2 cup melted butter
1 cup brown sugar
1/2 tsp salt

GLAZE

6 tbsp melted butter
1/2 cup milk
1/2 orange juice
2 pounds powdered sugar

CHAPTER 5: COOKIES!!!!

Oh, how I love cookies!

I have a large cookie jar on my counter and it always has homemade cookies in it. If it is ever empty my family is sure all is wrong in the world hahaha. I do my best to make sure there are always plenty of cookies in the jar. I love sharing cookies with others, it's the best way to spread love. All of these cookies recipes are easy and delicious. So get busy and share the love of cookies.

Simple Granola & Chocolate Chip Cookies

1/2 cup butter
1/2 vegetable shortening
3/4 cup brown sugar
3/4 granulated sugar
1 tbsp vanilla
2 eggs
2 cups flour
1 tsp baking soda
1 tsp salt
2 cups granola (oats, honey, raisins
and almonds is my favorite)
1 1/2 cups chocolate chips

Preheat oven to 350 degrees.

Cream butter, shortening, sugars, vanilla, and eggs. Then add flour, baking soda,
and salt and mix well. Add granola and chocolate chips. With a large scoop
put balls of cookie dough on cookie sheet and bake for 13-15 minutes.

ENJOY

Pumpkin Chocolate Chip Cookies

1 box spice cake mix
1 regular size can pumpkin puree 15-oz
2 cups chocolate chips

That is it!! Mix the cake mix and canned pumpkin together and add chocolate chips. Use large scoop and put on a cookie sheet and bake at 350 degrees for 13-15 minutes. These are my husband's favorite.

ENJOY

Fruit Cocktail Cookies

1/2 butter
1/2 vegetable shortening
1 cup brown sugar
1 cup granulated sugar
3 eggs
1 tsp vanilla
4 cups flour
1 tsp baking soda
1 tsp baking powder
1 tsp salt
1 tsp cloves
1 tsp allspice
1 tsp cinnamon
2 cans fruit cocktail, drained

Cream butter, shortening, sugars, add eggs and vanilla mix well. Add flour, soda, baking powder, salt, and the spices mix well. Then add well drained fruit cocktail and mix well. Bake at 400 degrees for 15 minutes.

I buy the fruit cocktail with the extra cherries because I like the red color they add to the cookies and the kids love cherries but any fruit cocktail works.

These cookies are soft and wonderful. My great grandmother made these for us as kids and I have never forgot them and love making them for my kids and so will you.

Chocolate Chip Cookies

1 cup butter softened
3/4 cup white sugar
3/4 cup brown sugar
1 tbsp vanilla
2 eggs
2 tbsp milk
2 3/4 cups flour
1 tsp salt
1 tsp baking soda
1 1/2 cups or 12 ounces of chocolate chips

Preheat oven to 350 degrees.

Mix butter, sugars, vanilla, eggs, and milk. Then add flour, salt, and soda mix well. Add chocolate chips, when all ingredients are well combined make into 1 inch balls and place on baking sheet. Bake for 10-13 minutes. These are best warm right out of the oven with a big glass of milk. Or you can do what my son Hunter does and take 2 out of the cookie jar and heat them up in the microwave for 15 seconds and they taste like they are right out of the oven.

These are Hunter's favorite cookie, plain chocolate chip cookies. I hope you love them as much as he does.

Soft & Fluffy Frosted Sugar Cookies

DOUGH

2 eggs
1 cup sugar
8 ounces cream cheese
4 cups flour
3 tsp baking powder
1 tsp salt
1 tsp vanilla

FROSTING

1/4 cup butter softened
1/4 cup cream cheese
3 cups powdered sugar
1 tsp vanilla
2 tbsp milk
Food coloring

Preheat oven to 375 degrees.

Whip eggs in large bowl of stand mixer until foamy, add sugar, mix well then add softened cream cheese, vanilla. When cream cheese is completely incorporated add flour, baking powder, and salt. Mix until dough forms then cover bowl with plastic wrap and refrigerate for 1 hour. Remove from refrigerator and roll out on floured surface. Use cookie cutters to cut into whatever shape your heart desires.

Place on a baking sheet with baking mat—this helps the bottoms stay light-colored. Bake for 8 minutes or until fluffy. Remove from oven let cool for 3 minutes on baking sheet then place cookies on cooling rack to cool completely.

Frosting: cream butter and cream cheese together. Add 1 cup of powdered sugar at at a time, then add milk, vanilla, and food coloring of choice.

Monster Cookies

1/2 cup butter
1/2 cup sugar
1/2 cup brown sugar
1/2 cup peanut butter
2 eggs
2 tsp vanilla
1 1/4 cups flour
1 1/4 cups old fashioned rolled oats
1 tsp salt
1 tsp baking soda
1 tsp baking powder
1 cup M&Ms candies
1 cup semi sweet chocolate chips

Preheat oven to 350 degrees.

Cream butter, sugars, peanut butter, eggs, and vanilla. In a separate bowl stir together flour, oats, salt, baking soda and powder. Add dry mixture to wet mixture. Then add M&Ms and chocolate chips. Using a big cookie scoop put dough in large scoops on baking sheet. Bake for 12-14 minutes. Remove from oven and allow to cool on pan.

These cookies are big and super good! My boys love these cookies. They are soft chewy and super filling. They are the perfect snack for the hungriest kids. But be prepared for the gallon of milk they will drink with them. HAHAHA

ENJOY

Peanut Butter Cookies

1/2 cup sugar
1/2 cup brown sugar
1/2 cup shortening
1/2 cup peanut butter
1 cup flour
1 tsp salt
1 tsp soda
1 tsp vanilla
1 egg

Preheat oven to 350 degrees.

Combine first four ingredients, then add other ingredients and mix well. I use a small melon baller to scoop out balls of dough. I put them on a baking sheet with a baking mat. I put the balls on the sheet them I make hatch marks on the top with a fork. Bake at for 8-10 minutes until all puffed up. Remove and cool on pan for 3 minutes and then move to cooling rack.

These cookies are soft and yummy. You can use creamy or chunky peanut butter. You can add 1/2 cup chocolate chips if you want. These are my favorite peanut butter cookies and everyone loves them they don't last long in the cookie jar.

No-Bake Chocolate Cookies

1/2 cup butter
2 cups sugar
1/2 cup milk
1/3 cup cocoa powder
1/2 cup peanut butter
2 tsp vanilla
3 1/2 cups quick cooking oats

In saucepan on stove top over medium heat melt butter add sugar, milk, cocoa, peanut butter, vanilla, and quick cook oats. Cook for 5 minutes stirring constantly. Remove from heat and scoop spoonfuls onto wax paper and cool.

ENJOY

CHAPTER 6: CASSEROLES
A Large Deep Dish Of Goodness!

A casserole is a tasty blend of hearty meats, vegetables, noodles, and sauces blended together baked in the oven and served in the same dish. I don't know about you guys but casseroles are dinner at my house at least a couple nights a week. They are fast, easy, filling, and delicious. I believe you can make almost any ingredients into a casserole and feed a crowd or in my case two big boys that can really put away the groceries. If you ask my kids what a casseroles main ingredient should be they would say cheese. I hope these recipes help you make easy dinners at your house.

Easy Lasagna

1 pound ground beef
1 package lasagna noodles
1 pound pork sausage
4 cups shredded mozzarella cheese
1 small yellow onion
2 cups cottage cheese
1 tbsp minced garlic
1 cup Parmesan cheese
1 jar spaghetti sauce
1 egg
2 tsp Italian seasoning
4 cups shredded cheddar cheese
1 tsp red pepper flakes
1 tsp salt
1 tsp black pepper

Preheat oven to 350 degrees.

In a large pot boil water with a pinch of salt and a splash of olive oil in it. Add noodles and boil according to package directions. Drain noodles and set aside.

In large skillet, brown ground beef and sausage with chopped onion, garlic. Add sauce, seasonings, salt & pepper. Simmer meat mixture on low.

In a bowl, mix mozzarella, cottage cheese, parmesan with the beaten egg.

In a large casserole pan, drizzle olive oil in the bottom, then arrange 3-4 noodles to cover bottom of pan in single layer. Spread 1/3 of the cheese mixture over noodles. Top cheese with 1/3 meat mixture. Then cover the meat mixture with 1/3 of shredded cheddar cheese.

Repeat layers two more times: noodles, white cheese mixture, meat mixture, cheddar cheese.

Cover with foil and bake for 40 minutes, then remove foil and bake 10 minutes more. Remove from oven and let rest 10 minutes, then dish up big squares of wonderful.

ENJOY

Chicken Enchiladas

2 cups shredded chicken
2 cups Colby Jack cheese
1 19-oz can green chile enchilada sauce
1 cup sour cream
1 cup chicken broth
8 large corn or flour tortillas
1 4.5-oz can chopped green chiles

Preheat oven to 350 degrees.

Cook 2 large chicken breasts in a large cast iron skillet with a little olive oil. When cooked shred in the skillet with 2 forks. Add cheese, enchilada sauce, sour cream, chicken broth, and chiles. Stir well over medium heat. When it begins to bubble, remove from heat.

Dip tortillas into mixture for a minute or so just to soften.

Spoon 1/4 cup of liquid out of the pan into the bottom of a 9x11 baking dish.

Scoop 1/2 cup mixture with a slotted spoon into each tortilla so you're getting mostly chicken and chilies. Roll them up and place them seam side down in the baking dish. Pour remaining liquid over enchiladas and top with remaining cheese.

Bake for 20 minutes.

These are easy, delicious, and a family favorite. I double this recipe often because my son Hunter loves these as leftovers.

ENJOY

Monterey Chicken

1/4 melted butter
1 cup smashed tortilla chips
1/4 cup flour
1 package or 2 tbsp taco seasoning
4 boneless chicken breasts
2 tbsp butter
1/4 cup chopped onion
1 tbsp flour
1 tsp salt
1 cup milk
1 tsp hot sauce
1 1/2 cups Monterey Jack cheese
1/2 cup sliced olives

Preheat oven to 350 degrees.

Dip chicken breasts in melted butter. Shake in a zip bag with smashed tortilla chips, flour, and taco seasoning. Coat chicken well and place in an 8x8 baking dish.

In a saucepan melt butter, add onion, flour, salt, milk, hot sauce, cheese, and olives. Pour over chicken and bake for 30 minutes.

(ENJOY)

Cheesy Hamburger Macaroni

1 tbsp olive oil
1 pound ground beef
1 tsp of salt & pepper
1/2 small onion diced
1 tbsp Worcestershire sauce
2 tsp minced garlic
2 cups elbow macaroni
4 cups water
2 tbsp butter
1/2 cup milk
3 1/2 cups shredded cheddar cheese

In large pot or dutch oven over medium heat cook ground beef in olive oil. Add onion, garlic, salt, pepper, and Worcestershire sauce. Cook for 3-5 minutes. Then add macaroni, water, butter, and milk. Cover and cook until macaroni is soft 8-10 minutes. Then add cheese and stir well. Remove from heat.

Hunter my son came up with this recipe and it has become our go to for a quick filling dinner on late nights after sports. I hope it becomes a favorite for your family too.

ENJOY

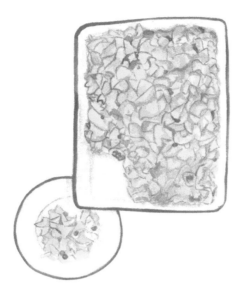

Tuna Noodle Casserole

1 can tuna, drained
1 tbsp butter
1/2 yellow onion, diced
1 can cream of mushroom soup
1 tsp diced garlic
2 dashes hot sauce
1 tsp salt & pepper
1 cup milk
4 cups cooked egg noodles
1 cup frozen peas
1 cup shredded cheddar cheese
2 cups crushed potato chips

Preheat oven to 350 degrees.

Spray 9x13 baking dish with nonstick spray. Cook egg noodles and set aside.

In skillet, melt butter, add onion, garlic, tuna and cook for 5 minutes.
Then add mushroom soup, milk, noodles, and frozen peas.

Pour into baking dish, top with cheese and then crushed potato chips. Cook
in oven for 25-30 minutes or until it is bubbly and slightly brown on top.

I grew up eating this a lot. It was one of my mom's
favorites. It is my go-to on Good Friday.

ENJOY

Tamale Pie

1 pound ground beef
1 medium onion chopped
1 clove garlic minced
1 tsp salt & black pepper
1 16-oz can kernel corn drained
1 16-oz can stewed tomatoes
1 8-oz can tomato sauce
3 cup water
1 tbsp chili powder
1 tsp cumin
1 2-oz can black sliced olives drained
1 large bag Frito corn chips
4 cups shredded cheddar cheese

Preheat oven to 325 degrees.

In a large skillet over medium heat, brown hamburger, add onion, garlic, and salt & pepper. Cook until onions are soft. Add corn, stewed tomatoes, tomato sauce, water, olives, cumin and chili powder. Stir well and simmer for 5 minutes.

In 9x11 baking dish put a layer of Fritos on the bottom of the pan followed by 2 cups of cheese. Then add meat mixture on top of that. Then add another layer of Fritos on top of that followed by the rest of the cheese.

Cover with foil for the first 30 minutes of baking, then remove foil and bake another 30 minutes. The top should be bubbly and chips soft.

This recipe is from a wonderful family friend, JoAnn. She is an amazing ranch cook and so was her mother. I was lucky enough to have JoAnn's daughter, Jodi, as one of my best friends growing up, so I ate JoAnn's delicious food often and this was my favorite. Oh, and she gave us saltine crackers with butter on them as a snack. Yummmmm. If you haven't tried it you must!

Thank you, JoAnn, for sharing this recipe with me. Much love.

ENJOY

Breakfast Casserole

32-oz bag frozen hash browns
1/2 cup melted butter
1 can cream of mushroom soup
1 cups sour cream
1 cup milk
4 eggs
1 pound breakfast sausage
1/2 yellow onion
1/2 green bell pepper
2 cups shredded cheddar
2 tsp salt
1 tsp pepper

Preheat oven to 350 degrees.

Brown sausage in skillet oven medium heat with onion and bell pepper.

Spread hash browns evenly in buttered 9x13 casserole dish.

In large bowl, combine melted butter, soup, sour cream, 1/2 cup
milk, 4 eggs, salt, pepper and cheese. Stir until combined.

Pour sausage mixture evenly over hash browns. Then
pour the soup mixture evenly over that.

Bake for 45 minutes or until the top starts to brown.

This is my favorite breakfast casserole recipe! It is delicious as dinner also, and
even better for brunch. It is so cheesy and delicious, it fills up tummies for sure.

Spaghetti Casserole

16 oz spaghetti noodles
2 tbsp olive oil
1 pound ground beef
1/2 onion diced
1 tbsp minced garlic
1 can of your favorite spaghetti sauce
1/2 teaspoon cinnamon
1/4 tsp nutmeg
2 tsp crushed red peppers
1 tsp sugar
1/4 cup red wine
1/2 cup Parmesan cheese

In a large dutch oven cook noodles according to package instructions. In large skillet brown beef, onion, and garlic. When the meat is brown and onions are soft, add sauce, spices, sugar, and red wine. Stir over medium heat until combined. Then turn to low and simmer for 5 minutes. Using a colander in the sink drain the water from noodles and then put them back into the pot. Pour the sauce mixture into the pot with the spaghetti. I use tongs to mix the sauce into the noodles. Once combined sprinkle top with parmesan cheese and serve.

This is my recipe for spaghetti and you can make in a flash for dinner and it tastes like you cooked it all day. My family loves it and often I double the recipe so we have lots of leftovers because my sons love leftover spaghetti for breakfast. HAHAHA. After all they are part Italian.

Sloppy Joe Casserole

1 package of 12 King Hawaiian Rolls
1 pound ground beef
1/2 onion diced
1/2 green bell pepper diced
4 tbsp minced garlic
1 8-oz can tomato sauce
1/4 cup ketchup
1 tsp mustard
1/4 cup brown sugar
2 tbsp Worcestershire sauce
1 tsp salt & pepper
1 tsp red pepper flakes
1 tsp chili powder
1/2 cup water
2 cups shredded cheddar cheese
1/3 cup butter
1 tbsp minced garlic
1 tsp Italian seasoning

Preheat oven to 350 degrees.

In a large skillet over medium heat, brown beef with onion, garlic, and bell pepper. When brown, add tomato sauce, ketchup, mustard, sugar, Worcestershire, spices, and water. Mix well and simmer for 5 minutes.

In a 9x13 baking dish, slice rolls in half and put the bottoms of the rolls in the baking dish. They should be snug. Spoon the meat mixture over the roll bottoms in pan. Top with cheese and put the tops of rolls over cheese pressing lightly.

Melt butter in small bowl, add garlic and seasoning, combine and brush on the tops of the rolls.

Bake for 15 minutes. Remove from oven and use a knife to cut around each roll and a spatula to serve them.

These messy, gooey, drippy, full of goodness Sloppy Joe Sliders are the bomb! After you eat Sloppy Joes this way, you can never eat them any other way. They will definitely become a family favorite. Just make sure you have plenty of napkins available when eating them.

CHAPTER 7:
CAKES & DESSERTS
Did someone say Cake?!?!

Ohhhh, the simple joy of cake. Cakes are a symbol of celebration, and my family and friends love to celebrate! Cakes are delicious way to spread love and cheer. I don't think a birthday, anniversary, or celebration of any kind is complete without a cake. I love to make cakes for the people I love and these recipes are some of their favorites.

Boozy Cake

CAKE

1 box cake mix (I use devils food or yellow)
1 small box instant chocolate or vanilla pudding
1/2 cup booze (rum or whiskey)
4 eggs
1 cup milk
1/2 cup vegetable oil

GLAZE

1/2 cup butter
1/2 cup sugar
1/2 cup booze (rum or whiskey)

Combine top six ingredients in electric mixer. Pour batter into a well greased Bundt pan. Cook for 40-45 minutes or until a toothpick comes out clean.

Let cake cool completely in the pan, then invert onto a large plate or platter. Then make the glaze. In a saucepan melt butter over medium heat, then add sugar and booze. Stir until sugar is dissolved and when it comes to a full boil, remove from heat and pour glaze over cake, coating all of it.

ENJOY

Ultimate Cheesecake

2 cups graham crackers
1/2 cup butter
1 tsp cinnamon
2 tbsp sugar
4 8-oz packages cream cheese
4 eggs
1 cup sugar
2 cups sour cream
1 tsp lemon juice
1 tbsp vanilla

Crush graham crackers up in food processor until you have 2 cups. Mix with melted butter, cinnamon, and sugar. Press mixture into the bottom of a spring pan and 1 inch up the sides.

Cream together softened cream cheese, sugar and eggs. Add sour cream, lemon juice and vanilla. Pour on top of graham cracker crust.

Wrap bottom of spring pan in tin foil and put inside of a baking pan. Pour some water in the bottom of the baking pan to create a water bath.

Bake at 350 degrees for 1 1/2 hours or until it's golden brown on top and a slightly wobbly center. Remove from oven and cool on wire rack for 20 minutes. Remove foil from bottom of pan, run a knife around the edges of the pan to loosen cheesecake. Cover with plastic wrap and refrigerate for 8 hours or up to 3 days. Remove cheesecake from refrigerator and spring pan. Serve and top with your favorite topping.

ENJOY

Carmel Apple Cake

CAKE

1 yellow butter recipe cake mix
1 small box vanilla instant pudding mix
1 cup water
4 eggs
1/2 cup vegetable oil
3 medium Granny Smith apples peeled and chopped

SAUCE

1/4 cup butter
1 cup brown sugar
2/3 cup sweetened condensed milk
1 tsp vanilla

Mix first 6 ingredients together with mixer. Pour into a 9x11 greased baking pan.
Bake at 350 degrees for 30-35 minutes or until a toothpick comes out clean.

Make caramel sauce: combine ingredients in a saucepan over medium heat
until bubbly. Pour over cake and let cool for 10 minutes before serving.

I serve this with vanilla ice cream or freshly whipped cream. I make
this cake at Christmas for my sister. It is a family favorite.

Vanilla Whipped Cream Cake

CAKE

1 cup heavy whipping cream
2 eggs
1 cup sugar
1 tbsp vanilla
1 3/4 cups flour
1/2 tsp salt
2 tsp baking powder

VANILLA FROSTING

1/2 cup butter softened
4 cups powdered sugar
2 tsp vanilla
1 tbsp tablespoons milk

Whip cream until stiff, add one egg at a time beat until fluffy. Add sugar and vanilla.

Sift together flour, salt, and baking powder in a separate bowl, then fold it into the cream mixture. Divide mixture into 2 round, well-greased and floured baking pans.

Bake at 350 degrees for 20-25 minutes or until a toothpick comes out clean. Cool on wire racks for 10 minutes. Then turn cakes out onto cooling racks to cool completely.

For frosting, cream butter in mixer, add powdered sugar, vanilla, and milk.

Put one cake on a plate and spread a thin layer of frosting on the top of it, then put the other cake on top and cover with remaining frosting.

You can serve this cake right away, but I prefer to refrigerate it for a couple hours or overnight, then serve it with vanilla ice cream.

OK, Karen, this is for you!!! Xoxo

Your favorite cake I ever made you for your birthday!
Friends like you only deserve the best!

Ruby's Carrot Cake

CAKE

2 1/2 cups flour
1 tsp soda
1 tsp salt
1 tsp cinnamon
2 cups sugar
3 eggs
1 tsp vanilla
1 1/2 cups vegetable oil
2 cups grated carrots
1 cup crushed pineapple
1/2 cup chopped nuts (pecans or walnuts)

FROSTING

1/4 cup butter
1 tsp vanilla
1 package softened cream cheese (4 ounces)
2 cups powdered sugar

Sift together dry ingredients in a bowl and set aside.

Cream together pineapple, eggs, vanilla, and oil. Add dry ingredients,
mix until combined. Then fold in carrots, and nuts.

Pour into 9x12 cake pan and bake at 350 degrees for 45-50 minutes or until a toothpick
comes out clean. Remove cake from oven and cool completely before frosting.

For frosting: cream butter, vanilla, cream cheese together. When light and
fluffy add powdered sugar. Pour over cooled cake and spread evenly.

This is my daughter Ruby's favorite cake for her birthday.

Rice Pudding

4 cups milk
4 eggs
1 cup sugar
1 tbsp vanilla
1/2 cup uncooked long grain rice
1/2 tsp salt
1/2 tsp nutmeg
1/2 tsp cinnamon
1/4 cup butter

In a 2- to 4-quart dutch oven on the stove top, bring rice and 2 cups of milk to a boil. Cover and simmer for 15 minutes or until liquid is absorbed and rice is tender. Remove from heat and stir in butter.

While that cools, in a large bowl whisk eggs, sugar, vanilla, salt and the rest of the milk until well combined. Stir into rice mixture. Sprinkle nutmeg and cinnamon on top of pudding.

Bake in 350 degree oven for 40-50 minutes. Remove from oven and stir well. Serve warm, or chill and serve later.

Chocolate Mayonnaise Cake

2 cups flour
1 cup sugar
2 tsp baking soda
3 tbsp cocoa powder
1 cup mayonnaise
1 cup water
1 tbsp vanilla

In a large bowl sift flour, sugar, soda, and cocoa powder. Add mayo, water, and vanilla. Pour into greased 11x9 baking pan. Bake in a 350 degree oven for 30 minutes or until toothpick comes out clean. Cool completely and frost with your favorite frosting.

This is Grandma Buzzetti's cake she makes for family dinners. It's a family favorite.

Bourbon Bread Pudding

CAKE

6 large eggs beaten
6 cups whole milk
2 cups sugar
12 cups cubed French bread
2 tbsp vanilla
2 tbsp Bourbon
1 1/2 cups semi-sweet chocolate chips

SAUCE

1/2 cup butter
2 cups brown sugar
2 cups half & half
1/2 cup Bourbon

Combine pudding ingredients in a large bowl and let stand for
at least 1 hour or up to overnight in the refrigerator.

Butter a large baking pan (10x14x2). Pour pudding into
pan and bake at 350 degrees for 50-60 minutes.

For sauce: melt butter in saucepan on medium-low heat, add brown sugar and stir
well. Stir in half & half. Heat through, stirring constantly until thick and bubbly,
then add Bourbon. Mix well and pour over pudding in pan. Serve immediately.

This recipe is so delicious. Who would have known chocolate and bourbon
could be so wonderful together. This recipe will feed a crowd. It is extra
delicious served with vanilla ice cream or fresh whipped heavy cream.

Sourdough Chocolate Cake

CAKE

1 cup sourdough starter
1 cup warm milk
2 cups flour
1 1/2 sugar
1 cup vegetable oil
2 tbsp vanilla
1 tsp salt
2 tsp baking soda
3/4 cup cocoa powder
3 eggs

FROSTING

6 cups powdered sugar
1/2 cup softened butter
1/2 cup or 4 ounces softened cream cheese
1 tbsp cocoa powder
1 tbsp hot water

Combine starter, milk, flour, and 1/2 cup of the sugar in mixing bowl. Let stand for 30 minutes.

Preheat oven to 350 degrees and grease a 9x13 baking pan.

In separate bowl, add remaining sugar, eggs, oil, vanilla, salt, baking soda, and cocoa. Gently combine the two mixtures. Mix well and pour into pan.

Bake for 30-35 minutes or until toothpick comes out clean when inserted into the middle of cake. Remove from oven cool completely then frost.

To make frosting: cream together butter and cream cheese. Add cocoa powder and hot water. Then add powdered sugar. Whip until light and fluffy. Pour on cake and spread evenly.

ENJOY

CHAPTER 8: MEAT

Where's the meat?!?

Living and growing up on a cattle ranch, beef was what was usually for dinner. My family doesn't consider it a meal if it doesn't include meat. For my husband nothing is better than a big ribeye steak medium rare. But my family and myself have many favorites so I will share them all with you.

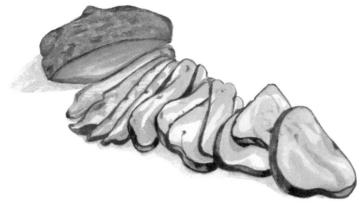

Tri-Tip

1 tbsp chili powder
1 tsp ground cumin
2 tsp salt
1/2 tsp ground red pepper
1 tsp ground thyme
1 tsp garlic powder
1 tsp onion powder
1 large beef tri-tip roast

Put all spices in bowl and mix well. Rub roast thoroughly with spice mixture. Let roast rest while grill preheats on high. Once grill is really hot, put roast on and sear on high on both sides then turn down to medium and cook for 45 minutes. Remove from grill and let rest for 5 minutes. Then slice and serve.

My son Anthony loves tri-tip. We hosted dinners for his high school football team and fed them tri-tip sandwiches. We would go through 13 to 15 large tri-tips to feed them. What can I say—they were growing boys. HAHAHA It was always great fun.

ENJOY

Meat Loaf

1 cup milk
6 slices white bread
2 pounds ground beef
1 cup Parmesan cheese
1 tsp salt
1 tsp course black pepper
1 tsp season salt
2 tbsp Italian seasoning
4 eggs beaten
1 package onion soup mix
1/2 cup ketchup
6 slices of bacon

SAUCE

1 cup ketchup
1/3 cup brown sugar
1 tsp mustard
1 tsp crushed red pepper

Preheat oven to 375 degrees.

Put milk in a large bowl, then tear up the bread into small pieces and let it absorb the milk. Add the ground beef, parmesan cheese, salt, pepper, season salt, Italian seasoning, eggs, onion soup mix, and ketchup. Mix together well with hands.

On a broiler pan, form mixture into a large loaf. Cut slices of bacon in half and lay them on top of loaf.

Mix all ingredients for sauce in small bowl. Pour half of the sauce on top of the meat loaf and cook in the oven for 45 minutes. Then pour the rest of the sauce on and continue to cook for another 15 minutes. Remove from oven and let rest for 10 minutes before cutting.

This meatloaf is full of flavor and will be a hit with everyone every time.

ENJOY

Brown Butter Bites

1/2 cup butter
1 pound bite size cubes of any red meat
salt & pepper

Heavily coat the meat cubes with salt & pepper. In a cast iron skillet over high heat melt the butter until it turns brown then add the meat cubes. Cook on high for 5 minutes, stirring several times. Meat should be nice and browned. Remove from heat.

Your family will eat these up faster than you can make them. I usually double this recipe—just add another cube of butter for every pound of meat. This is a great way to cook wild game meat, but it is delicious with beef also.

Stuffed Green Peppers

4 green bell peppers
1 pound ground beef
1 beaten egg
1/2 cup diced onion
1 tbsp minced garlic
1/2 cup breadcrumbs
1/2 cup ketchup

Cut the top of the peppers off and clean out the seeds.

Mix meat, egg, onion, garlic, breadcrumbs and ketchup in a bowl. Then stuff the peppers with the meat mixture.

Place the peppers in a baking dish and bake in a 350-degree oven for 1 hour. Take out of the oven and top with a little ketchup.

These are best served with mashed potatoes, in my opinion.

Baked Short Ribs

3 pounds short ribs
1/2 cup chopped onion
1 tbsp minced garlic
1/2 cup apple cinder vinegar
2 tbsp brown sugar
1 cup ketchup
1 tsp salt
1 tsp black pepper
1/2 cup water
3 tbsp Worcestershire sauce

Cover bottom of dutch oven with olive oil. Place ribs in dutch oven on cook top. Brown the ribs on both sides. Then mix the remaining ingredients in a bowl and pour over the short ribs.

Put the cover on the dutch oven and bake for 2 1/2 hours at 325 degrees.

Beef Wellington

ROAST

1 Beef tenderloin roast
2 tbsp butter
2 tbsp olive oil
1 tsp rosemerry & salt & pepper
1 red onion, chopped
2 tbsp minced garlic
2 1/2 cups chopped mushrooms
1/4 cup Italian breakfast sausage
1 tbsp Worcestershire sauce
1/4 cup breadcrumbs
1 box sheet puff pastry, thawed
1 egg

GRAVY

1 yellow onion, chopped
2 tsp thyme
2 tsp grape jelly
1/4 cup red wine
1 tsp Dijon mustard
2 1/2 cups beef stock
3 heaping tbsp flour
1 tbsp butter

Preheat oven to 425 degrees.

Heat olive oil and butter in large, cast-iron skillet over medium-high heat.

Rub beef tenderloin with rosemary, salt, and pepper. Put beef in pan and sear well on all sides. Remove beef from pan to a plate once seared.

Turn heat down to medium on skillet, add sausage, mushrooms, garlic, and onion. Stir together and cook until sausage is broken up and cooked, and onions are tender. Stir in Worcestershire sauce, add breadcrumbs to absorb excess moisture. Remove pan from heat and let cool while you prep puff pastry.

On a large sheet of flour-dusted parchment paper, roll out puff pastry sheet to 11x15 inches. Spread mushroom mixture onto the pastry, leaving a 2-inch gap around the edges. Whisk the egg up in a small bowl and brush egg wash on the edges of the pastry.

Set the beef tenderloin at one end of the pastry and roll up in the pastry. Pinch edges to seal shut. Coat pastry with egg wash.

Lift edges of parchment paper to transfer it and the roast to a baking sheet"Bake for 40 minutes. The center will be medium-rare with ends more well-done. Remove from oven and let rest for 5 minutes before carving.

For the gravy: use the same skillet used for mushroom mixture. Over medium heat, cook butter, onion, and thyme, stirring often until onions are soft. Then stir in jam, wine, mustard and flour. When combined stir in stock. Simmer until mixture starts to thicken. Then use an emulsion blender to liquify until there are no big chunks of onion. Keep warm until ready to serve.

Cut Wellington into 1-inch slices and top with gravy.

This is the family favorite on Christmas Day at my house. It is now requested every year and there might be mutiny if I made anything else. HAHAHA

Mississippi Roast

1 chuck roast
1 packet ranch dressing/dip mix
1 packet brown gravy/au jus mix
1 stick butter
6 Pepperoncini peppers
1 tsp salt & pepper
1 tsp garlic powder

Put roast in crockpot. Sprinkle ranch mix and gravy mix on top. Put cube of butter on top and place peppers around it. Pour a little of the pepper juice from jar in bottom of crockpot. Sprinkle salt, pepper, and garlic powder over the top.

Cook on low for 8-10 hours. Shred meat into juice and serve over mashed potatoes.

My oldest son, Anthony, loves this roast. I always try to make it for him when he is home from college.

Turkey

20-25 pound turkey

BRINE

1 orange cut in 4 pieces
1 cup kosher salt
1 cup whiskey
1 cup apple cider
1/4 cup maple syrup
1/4 cup brown sugar
1 tbsp peppercorns
1 bay leaf
1 clove garlic
1 sprig fresh rosemary
1 onion cut into 4 pieces
Water to cover turkey

STUFFING

1 box seasoned stuffing mix
1 box cornbread stuffing mix
4 oz Italian breakfast sausage
4 cups yellow onions diced
4 cups diced celery
5 cups chicken broth
1 cup melted butter
1 tsp rosemary
1 tsp thyme
1 tsp sage
1 tsp parsley
1 tbsp minced garlic

Mix all brine ingredients together in a clean 5-gallon bucket. Put turkey in bucket and add enough water to cover. Carefully lift turkey up slightly and put back down just to mix water with other brine ingredients. Cover top of bucket with foil and put in a cool place overnight.

The next morning, remove turkey from brine and rinse in the sink with cool water thoroughly. I pat turkey dry with paper towels. I then give it a thorough rub down with softened butter all over the outside and inside the body cavities. Then I sprinkle it with salt & pepper.

I make the stuffing and stuff the body cavities of the turkey. Start stuffing by browning sausage in a large skillet on the stove top over medium heat. Add butter to melt, then add onion, celery, and garlic cook until tender. Then turn off heat and add stuffing mixes, seasonings, and broth. Combine well, then stuff bird. Take the left over stuffing and put it in a covered baking dish and add it to the oven the last hour the turkey has to cook.

Put turkey in roaster oven, or conventional oven covered, at 325 degrees for 4 1/2 - 5 hours or until the tender timer pops up or the legs fall away from the body and it is golden brown. I do baste my turkeys every hour to keep them extra moist and flavorful. Before I put the turkey in the oven I pour a bottle of white wine and a can of chicken broth in the bottom of pan. Then every hour I take the lid off and quickly use my baster and suck the liquid up from the bottom of the pan and drench the bird with it. When the turkey is done I remove it from the pan and transfer it to a large cutting board where my husband carves it while I make the gravy.

GRAVY

4 tbsp butter
chicken broth
flour
salt & pepper
2 tbsp heavy cream

Pour contents of roasting pan into a large saucepan on the stove top. It's OK if there is a little stuffing or chunks of turkey in it, because you are going to use an emulsion blender to liquify it all and it will add flavor. Use your emulsion blender and blend liquid in saucepan until very smooth. Then add butter, and cream stir until melted.

Add 4 heaping tbsp flour into pot and use emulsion blender to thoroughly combine. Turn heat on medium under saucepan at this point. The gravy needs to come to a boil and thicken. Then add broth a little at a time until the gravy is the thickness you desire. Add salt & pepper to taste.

CHAPTER 9: PIE

A beautiful pastry filled with wonderful goodness!

Pies are the prefect end to a wonderful meal or the best beginning to the perfect day. Yes, I eat pie for breakfast sometimes as a treat. Banana cream is my favorite for breakfast. I can justify anything, trust me. It does have bananas and milk. hahaha

Pie Crust

1 1/4 cup flour
1 tsp salt
1 tsp sugar
1/2 cup cold butter or shortening
1/4 ice cold water

This recipe makes one pie shell. If you need a top for your pie, double this recipe.

In a bowl add flour, salt, sugar and mix well. Cube cold butter or shortening and add to flour. Combine with a pastry cutter until it's all crumbly with pea-sized pieces. Add cold water. I use a fork to mix water in. Work into ball and cover with plastic wrap. Put it in the refrigerator while you make the filling for your pie (30 minutes or so.)

Preheat oven to 425 degrees.

Dust pastry mat or work surface with flour and roll out with rolling pin in a circle at least 3 inches larger than the pie plate. Fold pastry in half and transfer to pie plate. Crimp edges and cut off excess pastry.

For precooked pie shell, bake for 10-15 minutes. Remove from oven and cool completely before adding filling.

For a baked pie, add filling, then roll out top crust and bake pie as directed.

This pie crust is delicious, flaky, and easy.

Blueberry Banana Cream Pie

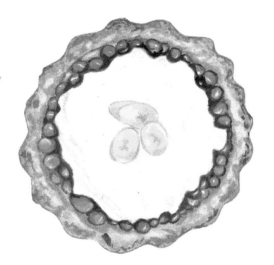

1 pre-cooked pie shell
2 bananas
1 cup powdered sugar
1 8-oz package cream cheese
1 regular container whipped topping
1 can blueberry pie filling

In pre-cooked cooled pie crust, layer sliced bananas to cover the bottom. I coat the bananas with a thin layer of lemon juice to keep them from turning brown.

Cream softened cream cheese and sugar in a mixer with whisk attachment until light and fluffy, then fold in whipped topping and pour on top of bananas. Chill in the refrigerator for 1 hour. Then remove from the refrigerator and top with blueberry pie filling.

This pie is one of my mom's favorites. It's delicious anytime of the year.

Rhubarb Pie

5 cups rhubarb cut into 1/2-inch pieces
1 1/2 cups sugar
4 tbsp flour
1/2 tsp salt
1 tsp lemon juice
1/2 tsp nutmeg
1 tsp vanilla
3 tbsp butter

Preheat oven to 350 degrees.

Mix all ingredients except butter in big bowl. Let it sit while you prepare the pie crust.

Stir filling ingredients again before pouring in pie crust. Dot with butter,
then put top crust on. Cut design in crust with pairing knife to vent, I always
do a heart. Use milk or egg wash on the top it makes the pie prettier.

Bake for 45-50 minutes.

This is my husband's favorite pie! He loves it. I try to make
it for him at least a couple times a year or so.

ENJOY

Pecan Pie

1 cup light corn syrup
3 large eggs
1 cup sugar
2 tbsp butter
2 tsp vanilla
1 1/2 cups chopped pecans
1 pie crust

Preheat oven to 350 degrees.

Mix all ingredients in a bowl and then pour in pie crust. Bake
for 50 minutes. Cool for 1 hour before serving.

I love this pie. I even have myself convinced its healthy. It has nuts and
eggs, lots of protein! HAHAHA. I have added 1/2 cup chocolate chips
and a shot of Bourbon to this recipe, to make it even more rich.

Banana Custard Cream Pie

FILLING

2/3 cup sugar
1/4 cup corn starch
1/2 tsp salt
3 cups milk
4 eggs
2 tbsp butter
1 tbsp vanilla
3 bananas

WHIPPED CREAM

6 tbsp powdered sugar
2 cups heavy whipping cream

Mix sugar, cornstarch, and salt in saucepan. Slowly stir in milk. Cook over medium heat stirring constantly until mixture thickens. Remove from heat.

Beat eggs slightly in glass bowl. Pour 1 cup of hot milk liquid from saucepan over eggs and whisk together. Then pour egg mixture into milk mixture. Stir for 1 minute. Add butter and vanilla. Press a piece of of plastic wrap to surface of pudding and put it in the refrigerator to cool.

While custard cools make your pie crust. When pie crust is cooling make the whipped cream. Slice the bananas and coat them with a thin layer of lemon juice so they don't turn brown. Place 2 sliced bananas in bottom of pie shell, put cooled custard on top, add whipped cream then top with last sliced banana. Refrigerate for at least 1 hour before serving.

Our family takes a snowmobile vacation to West Yellowstone Montana every year. There is the best breakfast place called Running Bear and it has been a long standing tradition to eat their banana cream pie for breakfast. This is my version of that amazing pie.

ENJOY

Pumpkin Pie

1 1/2 cups canned pumpkin
3/4 cup sugar
1/2 tsp salt
1 1/2 tsp cinnamon
1 tsp ground ginger
1/2 tsp nutmeg
1/2 ground cloves
3 eggs
1 1/4 cups milk
2/3 cups evaporated milk
1 -10 inch pastry shell

Preheat oven to 400 degrees.

Combine pumpkin, sugar, salt, and spices. Blend in eggs, and both milks. Pour mixture into pastry shell and bake for 15 minutes, then reduce temperature to 350 degrees and cook for another 35 minutes or until knife inserted in middle comes out clean. Remove from oven and cool completely. Serve with fresh whipped heavy cream.

No holiday is complete without pumpkin pie and this recipe is a family favorite. But my son Hunter has requested it for his birthday before and it's in August. So anytime is a good time for pumpkin pie!!!

ENJOY

CHAPTER 10: BREAKFAST
Rise and Shine!!!

I have cooked breakfast for my lucky children and husband almost everyday for the past 21 years. I don't even buy boxed cold cereal. But my kids have never minded, because they get eggs Benedict, sourdough pancakes, Belgian waffles, French toast, birds in a hollow, breakfast pizza, monkey bread, biscuits and gravy, and much much more. It is safe to say I love to cook breakfast. I think it is important to start your day with a full belly.

Eggs Benedict

poached eggs
Canadian bacon
Hollandaise sauce
English muffins
Paprika

Toast English muffins, top with warmed bacon, egg, cover in Hollandaise sauce and sprinkle lightly with paprika.

Simple simple simple don't make it hard. I bought an egg poacher for the microwave that poaches an egg in 1 minute. I also use the packaged Hollandaise sauce that you just add butter, milk, and a splash of lemon juice. It's easy and delicious. I have also used biscuits, topped with strips of bacon, scrambled eggs and Hollandaise sauce. Delicious!!! The possibilities are endless.

Eggs Benedict is my son Hunter's favorite breakfast. I got really good at making it quick in the mornings. It's not just a weekend favorite anymore.

Birds in a Hallow

Eggs
French bread

Cut a thick piece of French bread approximately 1 1/2 inches thick. Remove the center of the piece of bread. In a buttered skillet over medium heat, put the bread center and crust ring in the pan to toast. Crack an egg into the center of the crust ring. Sprinkle with salt and pepper. Cover the pan with a lid for 3-4 minutes, flip both over and cover for another 3-4 minutes or until bread is golden brown and egg is not visibly runny. Serve on a plate with bread center.

My kids use a fork to puncture the yolk and dip the bread center in and soak all its yummy goodness up. Then they just pick up the remaining ring and eat it up. Yum Yum!

ENJOY

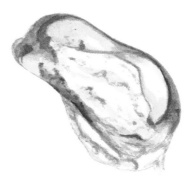

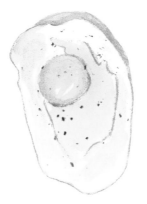

Belgian Waffles

2 cups flour
2 tsp baking powder
1/2 teaspoon salt
4 eggs separated
2 tbsp sugar
1 tsp vanilla
4 tbsp melted butter
2 cups milk

Preheat Belgian waffle maker. Sift all dry ingredients into a medium bowl and set aside. Separate egg whites and egg yolks into 2 separate mixing bowls. Add sugar to eggs yolks and stir until dissolved. Add vanilla, melted butter, and milk. Whisk until combined. Combined egg yolk mixture with flour mixture. Whip egg whites until soft peaks form. Then gently fold in egg whites to other mixture.

Coat waffle iron with non-stick spray and pour enough batter to cover waffle iron. Cook according to waffle iron directions.

French Toast

Any bread
4 eggs
1 cup milk
2 tsp vanilla
1 tbsp melted butter
1 tsp sugar
1/2 tsp cinnamon

Whisk all ingredients together well. Then dip any bread into the mixture (when I say any bread, I mean any bread—I have used leftover hot dog or hamburger buns, French bread) and cook on 350 degree, well-buttered griddle until both sides are until golden brown. Smother hot French toast with butter and syrup.

Breakfast Pizza

2 tablespoon vegetable oil
4 medium to large potatoes peeled and shredded
2 cups shredded cheddar cheese
3/4 cups sour cream
4 pieces of cooked bacon broken up into pieces
1 tsp dried chives

In a large nonstick skillet over medium heat, spread oil around pan. Spread shredded potatoes to cover the bottom of the pan, flatten out with a spatula. When golden brown on the bottom, flip over like a big pancake. Add cheddar cheese to the top of the hash browns. When the bottom of the hash browns are golden brown and the cheese is melted, remove from heat. Slide hash browns out of pan onto a big plate or plater. Cover cheese with sour cream, bacon, and chives. Cut into slices with a pizza cutter just like regular pizza.

THIS IS FOR YOU, KIERSTEN!!! AUNT TAM LOVES YOU!

Sourdough Pancakes

SOURDOUGH STARTER

4 potatoes
4 cups water
1 package dry yeast
2 tsp sugar
2 cups all purpose flour

BATTER

2 cups flour
3 tbsp sugar
1 cup warm milk or buttermilk
1 1/2 cup sourdough starter
2 eggs at room temperature
4 tbsp melted butter
1 tsp salt
1 tsp baking soda

Peel and cube potatoes, put them in a medium saucepan and add water. Bring to a boil over medium heat until the potatoes are fork tender about 15-20 minutes. Drain potato water into a medium sized bowl. Let potatoes cool and then put them into the refrigerator for mash potatoes later.

Once the potato water is just warm, add the sugar and stir until dissolved. Sprinkle yeast over water and stir gently. Let mixture rest for 5 minutes, then add flour and stir well with a wooden spoon until completely combined. Cover bowl with a towel and let sit in a warm, draft free place for 8-12 hours until mixture is full of bubbles.

You can use up to half of this starter right away or you can store it in a container in the refrigerator. Each time you remove starter from the refrigerator to use it, stir it well with a wooden spoon. If you use 1 cup starter, then replace it with 1 cup of flour, 1 cup of warm water and 1 tsp sugar. Mix into remaining starter and leave it out of the refrigerator with the lid off for 8 hours. Then put it back into the fridge with the lid on.

You must use your starter and feed it every two weeks to keep it fresh. Also avoid direct sunlight when leaving starter out of the refrigerator. I had a glass jar full of starter on the counter I had just fed. At some point during the day, it was in the sun and when I came home, it was all over the counter. It will expand greatly if it gets too warm.

For the batter: mix all ingredients together except the baking soda—fold it in after all other ingredients are mixed together. Let batter rest for 5 minutes. Then add large scoops of batter to a 350 degree, well-buttered griddle. Cook until both sides are golden brown. Best served hot off the griddle with butter and your favorite syrup.

Monkey Bread

BISCUIT DOUGH

To dough recipe on page 50, add
the following ingredients:

1/2 cup melted butter
1/2 cup white sugar
1/2 cup brown sugar
1 tbsp cinnamon
3/4 cup chopped pecans (optional)

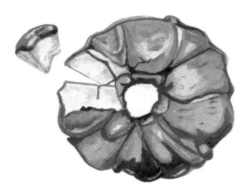

CARAMEL SAUCE

1/4 cup butter
1/2 cup light corn syrup
2/3 cup sweetened condensed milk
1 tsp vanilla

OK, this recipe is so easy and extra delicious. I use my biscuit dough recipe that is in the Breads & Biscuits part of this cookbook. Roll or pat dough out to 1-inch thick, and use donut hole cutter to cut the holes. (You can also use canned biscuits, biscuit mix, or thawed bread dough to make the holes.)

Melt the butter in a microwave safe bowl. In a different bowl, mix sugar and cinnamon together. Dip holes in the butter and roll them in the sugar and cinnamon.

In a saucepan over medium-low heat, melt butter, add brown sugar, corn syrup, and condensed milk. Stir until combined, then stir in vanilla.

Add nuts to bottom of a Bundt pan. Pour caramel sauce over nuts, add holes that have been dipped in butter and sugar mixture. Stack holes evenly around in the pan.

Bake at 375 degrees for 30-35 minutes or until top in golden brown. Remove from oven, let rest for 5 minutes, then turn out onto a plate or round platter. Let the pan rest upside down for a few minutes so all the caramel has time to run out over the bread. Remove pan—be very careful because caramel sauce will be very hot. Pull apart with a fork.

My entire family loves this recipe and requests it at every holiday get together.

Open-Faced Sandwich

French bread
Over-easy eggs
Mozzarella cheese
Basil

This is a super-flexible, easy, quick recipe. Cut the French bread in 1-inch slices. Put it under the broiler and toast on both sides. While bread is toasting, fry eggs in butter in a pan on the stove top. I sprinkle them with salt and pepper while cooking. You can cook your eggs to your liking, my family prefers over-easy.

Once your bread is toasted, pull it from the oven and butter one side. Put an egg on top of the buttered toast. Top with a slice of mozzarella cheese and sprinkle with basil. Put them back in the oven under the broiler until the mozzarella is melted.

Sometimes I add ham and tomatoes to this recipe. You can add anything else you would enjoy on a breakfast sandwich.

CHAPTER 11: SALADS
The Perfect Side Dish Every Time!!!

I think salad should be served with every meal. Yes, even breakfast. Jello salads are delicious at breakfast. Or a great Waldorf salad is sure to get you going. Some salads are a whole meal in one like taco salad. I am blessed that my kids like salads so they have been a constant in our meals. Salads always make me feel like I am eating healthy and serving healthy foods to my family. They are a great way to make fruits and veggies yummy!!!

Ribbon Salad

Two 3-oz boxes of your favorite flavor of red Jell-O
Two 3-oz boxes of lime Jell-O
One 8-oz package cream cheese softened
One 3-oz box of lemon Jell-O
3 cups mini marshmallows
1/2 cup pineapple juice
5 cups hot water

Add 2 1/2 cups hot water to a bowl and pour in the two packages of lime Jell-O. Very hot tap water works well, water shouldn't be boiling. Stir until Jell-O dissolves. Pour into glass 9x13 pan lightly sprayed with nonstick spray. Chill in refrigerator while preparing the next layer.

In stand mixer, mix softened cream cheese until light and fluffy. In a separate bowl, dissolve lemon Jell-O in 1 1/2 cups hot tap water and set in refrigerator to cool.

In a small saucepan over medium heat, add pineapple juice to marshmallows and stir constantly until melted and smooth. Pour into cream cheese mixture, mix on low until combined. Add the dissolved liquid lemon Jell-O to this mixture and mix well until very smooth, scraping sides of bowl often.

Once the green layer is firm, pour the cream cheese mixture over the top and put it back in the refrigerator to set up for at least 30 minutes.

Stir red Jell-O into 2 1/2 cups hot water until dissolved. Let cool for at least 30 minutes in refrigerator before slowly pouring over the set cream cheese layer. After adding the red layer, refrigerate for at least 1 hour before serving.

This was one of my mom's favorite recipes. It takes some time to make but is definitely worth it. It's a holiday classic and is timeless.

ENJOY

Frog Eye Salad

Two 15-oz cans mandarin oranges
One 20-oz can pineapple tidbits
1/2 cup pearl tapioca (not instant)
2 1/2 cups whole milk
3 large eggs, separated
1/2 cup sugar
1/2 tsp salt
1 tbsp vanilla
2 cups mini marshmallows
2 cups heavy cream
4 tbsp powdered sugar
2 tsp vanilla
6 Maraschino cherries halved

Pour oranges and pineapple in a strainer set over a bowl. Let drain in
the refrigerator while you make the rest of the salad.

Soak tapioca in 1 cup of water for 30 minutes, then drain but do not rinse. Set aside.

In a medium-sized heavy saucepan over medium heat, whisk together milk, egg yolks, sugar and salt. Add
tapioca and simmer, stirring constantly until thickened, then turn to low and simmer for 20 minutes, stirring
often. When the tapioca is translucent, it is fully cooked. Stir in vanilla. Remove from heat and let stand.

Whip egg whites until firm and gently fold in pudding. Pour into large bowl,
cover with plastic wrap and put it in the refrigerator to cool.

Whip cream until soft peaks form, add powdered sugar and vanilla. Remove fruit from
refrigerator and fold into whipped cream. Remove tapioca pudding from refrigerator
and fold the fruit mixture into the pudding. Dot the top with cherries and cover with
plastic wrap. Return to refrigerator for at least 1 hour or until ready to serve.

This is my favorite frog eye salad recipe. I have had it made many ways but this is
my favorite and it is gluten free! So my cousin Christy can eat it. It is creamy, rich,
and delicious. Once you try it you won't like it any other way either.

ENJOY

Italian Salad

SALAD

2 large heads of Romaine lettuce
1/4 red onion sliced very thin
1/2 cup Salami sliced thin
1/2 cup black olives
1/2 cup green olives
8 Peperoncini peppers
1/2 cup shaved provolone cheese
1 1/2 cups cherry tomatoes
1 cup croutons
1/4 cup sunflower seeds or pine nuts

DRESSING

1/2 cup olive oil
1 tsp minced garlic
1/4 cup red wine viegar
1 tbsp grated Parmesan
1 tsp Italian seasoning
1 tsp salt & pepper

Chop up lettuce and put in large bowl. Add sliced onion, salami, olives, peppers, cheese, tomatoes, croutons, sunflower seeds or pine nuts. Put all ingredients for dressing in a shaker bottle, shake it well and pour dressing on top of salad and toss well.

This is one of Grandma Buzzetti's favorite recipes. There used to be at an Italian restaurant that our friend Jason owned that we frequented, but he moved away and we missed his salad, so we recreated it and eat it at many family get-togethers.

7-Layer Salad

1 head of iceberg lettuce
1 cup frozen peas
2/3 cup mayonnaise
2 salad onions chopped
1 tbsp sugar
1/2 cup celery
2 hard boiled eggs sliced
1/4 cup Parmesan cheese
2/3 cup crumbled bacon

Chop up iceberg lettuce put in bottom of bowl. Add peas, spread mayo over top of peas and sprinkle with sugar and Parmesan cheese, then top with onions, celery, eggs, and bacon in layers. You can cover and leave in refrigerator for up to 24 hrs before serving. To serve, toss all ingredients well.

There are a lot of variations of this recipe but this is my favorite. My husband likes it because it doesn't have tomatoes, and he is Italian! Don't ask me? HAHAHA

ENJOY

Taco Salad

1 pound ground beef
1/2 yellow onion
1 tsp minced garlic
1 tsp salt & pepper
1 tbsp taco seasoning
2/3 cups water
1 head iceberg lettuce
1 can kidney beans drained and rinsed
1 large tomatoes chopped
1 cup shredded cheddar cheese
3 cups nacho Doritos
2/3 cup Catalina dressing

Cook ground beef in large skillet over medium heat, add onion, garlic,
salt & pepper, taco seasoning, and water. Simmer for 5 minutes or
until onions are translucent. Remove from heat and cool.

Chop lettuce and put in large bowl, add beans, tomatoes, cheese, Doritos coarsely
crushed, then top with meat mixture and dressing. Toss salad until combined.

My Aunt Diana and my mom made this all the time for us growing up.
It is delicious and easy. Kids love it, of course— it has Doritos in it.

Waldorf Salad

1/2 cup mayonnaise
1 tbsp lemon juice
1 tbsp sugar
2 apples red or green coarsely chopped
1 cup celery coarsely chopped
1/2 cup walnuts coarsely chopped
1/2 cup raisins

In large mixing bowl add mayo, lemon juice, and sugar. Mix well. Add apples, celery, walnuts and raisins. Stir with a spatula so all ingredients are coated with dressing from bottom of bowl. Serve immediately or cover with plastic wrap in the refrigerator for up to an hour.

This is one of my favorite recipes! I love it! I usually have all the ingredients on hand so its easy to whip up in a hurry. My daughter, Ruby, loves this salad and requests it often.

Nevada Salad

2 heads iceberg lettuce
1 cup mayonnaise
1 hard boiled egg
1/3 cup olive oil
2 tsp minced garlic
2 tbsp red wine vinegar
2 tsp salt
1 tsp pepper

Chop lettuce and put in large bowl. In medium bowl, add mayo, egg sliced, oil, garlic, vinegar, salt & pepper. I use my emulsion blender to mix all ingredients until smooth, but you can use a blender or food processor also. Pour dressing on lettuce and mix well. This salad has a lot of dressing on the lettuce—it is meant to be that way so enjoy. Add more salt and pepper if needed. Serve immediately.

This is a garlicky delicious salad that is served at the Basque dinner houses in our county. It is fast and simple and delicious. My sister requests it for dinners at my house, or when I come cook at her house. I am sure it will become one of your family favorites.

ACKNOWLEDGMENTS

Tom Baker: Cowboy Artist